CAN YOU FIGHT OFF AN ASSAILANT POISONED BY DRUGS OR ALCOHOL—AN ASSAILANT WHO HAS NO CONSCIENCE, HAS TREMENDOUS STRENGTH, AND FEELS NO PAIN?

Yes, you can—regardless of your sex,
size, age, or strength!

YOU CAN FIGHT BACK MENTALLY

Your mind is your most powerful weapon! Breathe deeply, walk assertively, and look directly at what is frightening you.

YOU CAN FIGHT BACK VERBALLY

If you know you're being followed, turn around and use commanding, vulgar words to startle the stranger.

YOU CAN FIGHT BACK PHYSICALLY

Never fight physically for your possessions—only for your life! Breathe deeply to control your adrenaline, and roar to increase your strength and confidence. Strike with the intention of causing serious injury, not just pain.

SURVIVE
DON'T BE A VICTIM

Debbie Gardner

WARNER BOOKS

A Warner Communications Company

Warner Books Edition
Copyright © 1982 by Debbie Gardner
All rights reserved.
This Warner Books edition is reprinted by arrangement with the author.

Warner Books, Inc., 666 Fifth Avenue, New York, NY 10103
Ⓦ A Warner Communications Company.

Photographs and illustrations by Fred Thoman

Book design by Richard Oriolo

Printed in the United States of America
First Warner printing: September 1984
10 9 8 7 6 5 4 3 2 1

Library of Congress Cataloging in Publication Data

Gardner, Debbie.
  Survive: don't be a victim.

  1. Self-defense. 2. Self-defense for women. I. Title. GV1111.G34
1984   613.6'6   84-2377
ISBN 0-446-38061-X (pbk.) (U.S.A.)
    0-446-38062-8 (pbk.) (Canada)

ACKNOWLEDGMENTS
My sincere thanks and appreciation are extended to
two of the finest families on earth,
THE GARDNERS and THE HERBERTS

the men who posed in the photographs:
MIKE GARDNER
BOB GARDNER
KEN HERBERT
FRED THOMAN

the thousands of women and men who attended
SURVIVE classes, lectures, and seminars
to further their safety and the safety
of their loved ones.

THIS BOOK IS DEDICATED TO
MY HUSBAND AND MENTOR

MIKE GARDNER

WHO IS THE SOURCE OF MY
INSPIRATION AND CONFIDENCE.

CONTENTS

FOREWORD

When I was twenty-seven years old, I was violently and brutally raped. My life was shattered overnight.

Nine years later, after a long and painful struggle and recovery, I came forth to speak as a rape victim. At this time in my life, I met Debbie Gardner and found in her a dear and wonderful friend. We touched each other's lives. My story reinforced her convictions as to the importance of teaching women how to protect themselves against a confrontation with an attacker. No woman is safe from rape! Therefore, no woman can afford not to read this book. The information and self-defense techniques in *Survive—Don't Be a Victim* are inherent to a person's survival if and when attacked.

Thank you Mike and Debbie Gardner for your time, your efforts, and your dedication in writing this book in order to prepare me, my loved ones, and many readers to fight effectively for our lives.

God bless you,
Pam Stump

INTRODUCTION

Thanks for caring enough about yourself to read this book. The purpose of writing it is to equip you with simple, effective fighting principles that you will remember all your life!

When I ended my eight-year career as a deputy sheriff patrol officer, I vowed that my new career as a mother and homemaker would include sharing with others my insight into self-defense and self-confidence.

Because of my former career and the fact that I am a woman of small stature, I know what it is to be scared! I know what it is to be challenged! And I know what it takes to **SURVIVE!** Because my safety depended on it, I have spent thousands of hours thinking and reading about self-defense, and I teach the basic principles of self-defense with my husband, who is also a police officer.

My research and experience qualify me to write confidently on this subject. I know there are several other books published on self-defense, but I assure you this book is different! *SURVIVE—Don't Be a Victim* is not just a "how to" book like all the others; it is also a "why" book. Section after section, I take the time to explain the "whys" of basic self-defense principles such as:

3

- Why **FEAR IS GOOD**
- Why you **FREEZE** when you are scared
- Why you must avoid **TUNNEL VISION**
- Why you must protect your **SPACE**
- Why **ROARING** is more valuable than screaming
- Why you should trust your **ADRENALINE**
- Why some **VITAL TARGETS** are more effective to strike than others
- Why you must strike an attacker to cause **INJURY** and not just **PAIN**
- Why a **HANDLE** on your keys (Kubotan®) is an effective self-defense weapon
- Why your attacker may be using that gun just as a **THREAT** and not as a **WEAPON**

Understanding these and other fighting principles is just as valuable as physically practicing one self-defense technique after another. It is a shame that the general public is brainwashed into thinking that unless they train physically for months or even years they cannot be effective in diverting or fighting off an attack. My experience in police work proved to me that it is people's **MINDS** that make them dangerous and not the number of hours they train.

The underlying purpose in writing this book is to encourage you to develop an **ANIMAL** in your personality. This animal is the mean, vicious, violent side of you that never surfaces until you feel challenged. Then, without hesitation, the polite, considerate, loving side of you turns "off" and your animal turns "on." Imagine a pet dog—a tame, loving animal that sits on laps and plays with children every day. When the wrong person comes to the front door at the wrong time of day, that tame pet becomes a vicious animal ready, willing, and able to chew up the intruder!

Read this book carefully and "feed" its content to the animal in your personality. Knowing that your animal exists will raise your confidence considerably.

Because I believe that it is your mind that makes you dangerous along with the development of an animal in your personality, I do not believe your gender, size, age, or strength has anything to do with your ability to protect yourself!

This book will not bore you with statistics. One assault, one rape, one murder, is one too many! Violence is an ugly topic, and some of the ideas you read, as well as the language itself, might be upsetting. It is not my intention to be crude or disrespectful. I just feel it is time for this topic to be presented openly and honestly.

SURVIVE is written in three sections, each explaining a different phase of "fighting." The first two sections, "Fighting Back Mentally" and "Fighting Back Verbally," stress **preventing** an attack. The third, "Fighting Back Physically," will teach you how to **survive** an attack. A fourth section, "Who Really Wins?," gives you advice on how to give an accurate description of your attacker to the police.

FIGHTING BACK MENTALLY

Does that word "fighting" bother you? Why? Is it because you've never been in a fight before? Is it because you think you are too small and too weak to fight effectively? Or is it because you secretly fear a legal system in which you, the innocent victim, would have to **prove** you acted in self-defense? Ahh...the truth is coming to the surface. The legal system of our country scares you to death, doesn't it? Well, it figures that you are probably a decent, law-abiding citizen who respects and upholds the law. All good people feel as you do! We squirm just driving past our local courthouse. We stiffen up every time we pass a police car—and for no good reason!

Why are we so frightened by the mere thought of it all, when criminals couldn't care less about the legal system and often laugh at the seriousness of being arrested?

Are criminals really intimidated by police, courts, and judges? Of course not! Their overall disrespect and inside knowledge of how to get around the law is astounding!

Deep in your heart, you recognize that our criminal justice system is far from just. It often appears that criminals have more rights than innocent victims.

Deal with this problem by adjusting your thinking:
- Being involved in the court system is a frightening experience, but when you are right, don't be afraid to prove it. The court system really is looking for truth and fairness. Stand tall...speak loudly...speak confidently and tell the whole honest truth, without one speck of hesitation!
- You have the right to protect your life and the lives of your family at all times. Only **you** know when your life is in danger. Just be sure you live to have your day in court.

FIGHTING BACK MENTALLY is essential for surviving or possibly preventing an attack. Remember the last time your phone startled you by ringing in the middle of the night? I bet the initial reaction you had to the first ring was "AUGHHH" and there you were...HOLDING YOUR BREATH...PARALYZED! As you searched for the courage to answer the phone, your heart beat loudly and the palms of your hands began to sweat.

It took all the strength you could gather just to spit out the word "Hello?" Why? Because you were afraid...but afraid of what? The present...the ringing of the phone? Or did you fear the future... the conversation on the phone, possibly news of an accident or death in the family? Generally speaking, we seldom fear the present, that which is happening now. We tend to fear what is going to happen next, the unknown. So when it comes to **fighting mentally,** always start by forcing yourself to breathe deeply and concentrate on what is happening right now! Handle what might happen next...later.

FEAR IS GOOD! DON'T BE AFRAID TO BE AFRAID! The fear you experience when you are frightened is good because fear brings on survival instincts. Biochemical reactions in your body take place in the form of an adrenaline pump. Adrenaline, in nonscientific terms, is boundless energy. You must recognize, however, that adrenaline cannot be turned on or off at will. It only comes upon you when you are frightened, whether you want it or not. It is adrenaline that makes your heart pump wildly and the palms of your hands sweat. When this happens, you must make a choice. You can hold your breath and allow this adrenaline pump to freeze you into stiffness, or you can turn this energy into immeasurable strength.

Breathing

Breathing is essential to controlling adrenaline. Without breathing, this energy cannot be released and causes a bottled-up, stiff reaction in your body. The second you breathe and allow this energy to escape from your body, you will find yourself stronger than you've ever been before!

I'm sure you've heard success stories about super-human feats that were performed by everyday people under extreme stress. One such story is about a woman who accidentally backed over her toddler in the driveway. She then lifted the car off him, kicked his body to safety, and saved his life. This woman truly concentrated the power of her mind (her desperate desire to save her child's life) in the muscles of her body. The end result was spectacular and not likely to be repeated in her lifetime. Hers was a decision of life or death...no other thought in mind except the act she needed to perform. Her child would be dead had she stood there frozen, holding her breath in horror.

If you really believe in the power of your adrenaline, then you should **never be afraid to be afraid** anymore! The lesson to be learned here is that **YOUR MIND IS POTENTIALLY THE MOST POWERFUL WEAPON OR FORCE YOU HAVE.** Your mind controls the strength of your muscles. Your muscles have no control over your mind. Your mind works **only** if you are breathing.

Continued deep breathing feeds your nervous system with oxygen so that you can think and react soundly. You cannot scream, run, or fight if you are not breathing.

Tunnel Vision

Fighting back mentally goes beyond just breathing. Can you relate to the following situation? You were walking in a parking lot, minding your own business, when all of a sudden you heard something behind you. Did you walk in TUNNEL VISION? You know what I mean—your heart beating wildly and your eyes locked straight ahead. You hunched your shoulders slightly and walked like a robot, holding your breath and praying that whatever was behind you would disappear.

Go on and admit it...you know exactly what I am talking about. I beg you, from this day forward, **NEVER WALK IN TUNNEL VISION AGAIN!** If

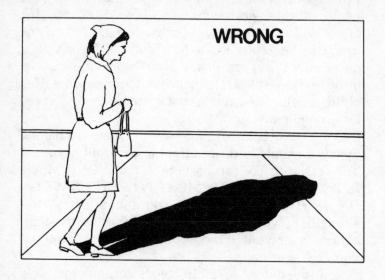

there is a potentially dangerous person around you, your body language will immediately show him how frightened you are. Think about it! Even before he breaks the law and attacks you, your body is showing him that you are an easy victim and that you are scared to death. This may be just the signal he needs to go ahead and follow through with the attack. Until he saw your reaction, maybe he was just looking you over to see whether you might be easy prey. He's looking for a victim, not a hassle. If you can improve your body language and project the image of a fighter (praying to God that you'll never have to back it up with action), chances are

you can divert this attack. Fighting back mentally
by avoiding tunnel vision is worth a try.

To avoid TUNNEL VISION you must:

- Recognize the feeling of adrenaline pumping
  in your body and **breathe** to control it
- **Walk assertively** with your shoulders straight
  up (a natural response when breathing deeply)
- Clench both your hands into **tight fists** (one
  hand should be armed with your keys)
- **Turn** and look directly at what is frightening
  you! (Is that hard? You bet! Don't look just
  once, look again and again and again. If it really
  is a person behind you, make eye contact!)

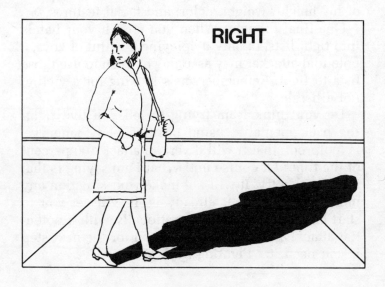

RIGHT

Postitive body language is essential to fighting
back mentally because:

- You know exactly whom you are dealing with —a real live dangerous person or a harmless animal using the same path as you.
- You are displaying your confidence and courage because it takes guts to face up to what frightens you. These are traits a potential attacker is not interested in seeing in a victim.
- You may arouse the curiosity of potential witnesses who are attempting to understand why your head is turning so strangely . . . back and forth . . . back and forth. . . .

A potential attacker would prefer to alarm you and catch you off guard. When you turn and look at him, he's not going to like the idea that you are able to describe him. The last thing he needs is the survivor of an attack giving an accurate description of his height, weight, color, and facial features.

One final thought: When you clench your hands into tight fists, openly displaying a fistful of keys, a potential attacker may assume you plan to use those fists to fight. Remember, he's looking for a victim, not a hassle.

Do you think I am trying to tell you that fighting back mentally, using positive body language, is foolproof, that it will divert an attack 100 percent of the time? Of course not! What I am saying is that it is worth a try. It will not make your situation any more serious than it already is. It **will** get you to start breathing and dealing rationally with a potential attack, and it **will** prepare you for the next step if you need it: "Fighting Back Verbally."

FIGHTING BACK VERBALLY

Does the idea of talking in a stressful situation frighten you? Be honest with yourself. Just how comfortable are you in a one-to-one conversation? On a daily basis, talking to family or close friends, I bet you do just fine. What about mere acquaintances or total strangers?

- Have you ever been so nervous that you stutter or spit just trying to complete a simple sentence?
- Have you ever avoided giving your view on a particularly emotional issue because you were sure that you would start crying?
- Have you ever choked up or been close to tears because someone disagreed with you or totally challenged your opinion?
- Have you ever felt uncomfortable talking with members of the opposite sex...for no apparent reason?

Well, don't feel bad. These reactions are quite common. I have experienced them all; therefore, I understand how difficult it is going to be for you to apply the principles listed in "Fighting Back Verbally." But you must trust me! Fighting back verbally can be a tremendous deterrent to preventing an

attack. As difficult as fighting back verbally with a potential attacker might be, I guarantee you that it is much easier than physically fighting him should his initial approach lead to an attack. To help you overcome your fear of talking to strangers, let me remind you to call upon your **ANIMAL** for help. Remember, I am encouraging you to deliberately develop that hidden, defensive personality that will do your verbal fighting for you! Before I list the principles, I need to impress upon you the value of understanding your **SPACE.**

Space

I'm sure that you know you are permitted to protect your body at all times, but did you know that you are also permitted to protect your **space**—that area immediately around your body, twenty-four hours a day, seven days a week? Think of it as elbow room. Keep in mind that sometimes you voluntarily give up your space in places like crowded elevators or jam-packed stadium events. Other than those occasions, the area within your arms' reach is **your space.** Be aware that the amount of your space depends on where you are.

> Example: Walking to the employee parking lot at quitting time, you may have only elbow room because everyone is walking in the lot at the same time. But if you work overtime and yours is the last car in the lot, the **space** of that entire lot is technically yours!

Consider the fact that in most cases, you cannot be beaten, robbed, raped, or murdered unless someone gets into your **space.** (An exception is an armed gunman who shoots you from across the parking lot, in which case all the self-defense in the world would not help you.)

You can best protect yourself by understanding how an attacker works his way to get into your **space.** The attack generally will happen in one of these three ways. (Each will be discussed later in detail.)

1. He may walk up to you casually, using a nonthreatening approach, and ask you what appears to be a simple question. While you are distracted, he will attack.
2. He may follow you, keeping his distance until he's sure you are vulnerable; then he will move into your space rapidly and attack.
3. He may hide, giving you no warning that you are in danger—then attack.

From experience and research I am convinced that the most common of these three attacks is the **casual, nonthreatening approach.** Unfortunately, most peo-

**HE MAY WALK UP TO YOU CASUALLY,
ASKING YOU A QUESTION....**

ple are unaware that this approach puts them in any danger. That is why I am going to emphasize that you become particularly aware of this potentially dangerous situation. Chances are you have experienced an approach of this type. I hope it didn't develop into an attack.

Example: You are all alone, walking to your car or outside a store, it doesn't matter. All of a sudden a stranger walks up to you and asks you a question. The question may be as harmless as his initial approach. It may vary from asking for the time, directions, or even items out of your purse or pocket, such as matches, cigarettes, tissues, change, a pen, and the like. (Strangers know that women are likely to accommodate their request without hesitation. There is something about women, maybe their maternal instinct, that makes them feel obligated to "help" whenever they can.)

So there you are, somewhat nervous about his presence but relieved when he asks you that "innocent" question. Thinking that you are safe, you reach into your purse or pocket and— Oh, God! He just put a gun in your back!

What went wrong? When he walked up to you, did you telegraph your fear through **poor body language**—not making eye contact, "jumping" at his initial approach, squeaking your reply to his question, or even apologizing to him by saying, "Oh! I'm sorry.... You scared me!"? Without realizing it, your body's reactions told him that you would probably be an easy victim. You did not fight back mentally or verbally. Your only choice was to submit or fight physically.

In this example, or in any situation where a

stranger walks up to you casually and asks an "innocent" question, follow these principles of "Fighting Back Verbally":

- **Make direct eye contact**
- **Protect your space**
- **Give a confident, negative reply** to his request such as:

> "I don't know.... My watch is broken."

> "No matches.... I don't smoke."

> "No, I don't know how to get to Main Street."

Make these statements even if your watch **does** work, you **do** smoke, and you **do** know directions to Main Street.

Consider the dangerous mistakes you make if you disregard these principles and decide to accommodate the stranger's request:

- You allow yourself to be **mentally distracted.** Instead of concentrating completely on why he is around you, you direct your thoughts to accommodating his needs:

> "Wait a minute.... Ummm... the time is seven-thirty."

> "Let's see, I know I have matches here somewhere...."

> "Hmmmm... the best way to Main Street is ..."

- You allow **your hands to be tied up.** Instead of allowing your hands to be free to fight or protect yourself, they are performing a service for the stranger:

"adjusting" the face of your watch
"digging" for matches
"pointing out" the direction of Main Street

- You allow **your eyes to move off the stranger.**
  Instead of keeping your eyes directly on him,
  you look away in order to accommodate his
  need:

  "looking down" at your watch
  "looking down" into your purse or pocket
  "looking toward" Main Street

These dangerous mistakes add up to your being
totally distracted by the stranger, allowing him ample opportunity to startle you with a weapon. A
common response from victims who live through this
type of attack is: "I swear I did not see that gun until
it was in my back. I don't know where it came from."

It is not my intention to make you paranoid or
uneasy with every stranger you encounter. Don't
take me out of context! I am referring to times when
you are all alone and your intuition tells you something is wrong. Make sure you remember how easily
you can be "set up" by a stranger pretending to
need your assistance.

There are reasons why an attacker would prefer to
approach you in this casual, nonthreatening way:

- **He gets to look you over and test your response
  before he attacks.** If your body language displays fear and intimidation and your voice
  squeaks when you respond to him, he can easily
  decide to attack. However, if your body language
  displays confidence and determination and
  your voice is clear and authoritative, he's likely
  to reconsider his attack upon you, choosing to
  look for a weaker subject. Remember, he's
  looking for a victim, not a hassle. By asking

you that "test" question, he has not broken the law. Even if you are suspicious of his intentions, you cannot have him arrested.

- **He has the opportunity to stand in your space.** Think about it. When a stranger approaches you and asks you a question, does he stand across the parking lot or on the other side of the room? No! More than likely, he is standing right at your side...within arm's reach...in your space! That is a good position for him should he decide to attack you.

I hope you now understand why I feel it is so important to stress the dangers of accommodating strangers. I hope you are convinced that the best way to handle the situation is to fight back verbally with a negative reply, thereby disrupting his game plan.

Talking "coldly" and "lying" to a stranger may make you feel bad, but you'll get over it. To make you feel better, do something special for someone you love...someone who deserves your trust; then give yourself credit for not allowing something tragic to happen to you!

The terror of being followed...you'll never really understand how horrible it is until it happens to you. What are your options? Consider them all—QUICKLY!

- Are there people around you? Good! Catch up to the crowd and get some help.
- Is there a store nearby, open for business? Great! Get in there and get some help.
- Are you in an isolated area with no stores or crowds to protect you? Then your options are limited. BREATHE DEEPLY and THINK! Keep

HE MAY FOLLOW YOU....

looking over your shoulder. Make sure you are
fighting back mentally with positive body
language.

- Can you run? Wait! Make sure there is a safe
place to run to. Otherwise, you will be wasting
valuable energy needed to fight physically for
your life.

Assuming none of these options is available to
you, fight back verbally by using these principles:

- **Immediately confirm your suspicion by making a deliberate change in your walking path.**
If the suspected attacker also changes his path
to continue following directly behind you, consider your suspicions accurate! He has just
committed himself to following you.

　　Examples: If you think you are being followed as you walk down the street, abruptly
cross the street. Look over your shoulder....
Did he follow you?

　　If you are in an open area such as a parking lot, deliberately zigzag between a few
cars. Turn and look....Did he follow your
strange path?

Your abrupt action should make him change his
mind and decide **not** to attack. If the situation does
not stop there, and he does continue following you:

- **Turn suddenly and look him in the eyes....**
- **Point your finger at him and ask him a direct
question,** such as:

"What the FUCK do you want?"

"What the HELL are you doing?"

"Are you following me, you SON OF A
BITCH?"

It is likely that you will startle him. Be prepared for a variety of responses:

- He'll be caught totally off guard, will change his mind about furthering the attack, and will flee the area.
- Maybe he'll stand there, dumbfounded, then try to explain his actions as "coincidental" or "harmless." DON'T BELIEVE HIM! Using strong language, insist that he keep his distance from you. Then walk to your destination, keeping your eyes on him at all times, of course.

There are many reasons why this type of verbal fighting is effective:

- **Your confidence is obvious to him.** He can't help but acknowledge the courage it took for you to turn and face him.
- **You talked first.** In any stressful situation, it is usually the person who "breaks the ice" who dominates the outcome of the conversation.
- **You pointed your finger at him.** Pointing your finger indicated your dominance and his subordination. (This is a form of persuasive body language that nuns have been using for years.)
- **You asked him a question.** Questions demand answers! For a short period of time, he's going to be mentally confused while deciding whether or not he should answer you. He is vulnerable when he hesitates, and his feeling of vulnerability will lower his confidence.
- **You spoke with vulgar, commanding words.** Vulgarity is important! Please forgive me for being crude, but remember that I am being honest! You can be sure that a potential attacker

understands exactly what you are saying when you "curse." You are speaking HIS language! Vulgar words work side by side with positive body language in "painting" an outside image of you: YOU ARE DANGEROUS! (Inside, of course, you acknowledge your fears and know that you are putting on a front in order to save your life. What you've done is reverse the CON.... YOU CONNED HIM!) Think about the alternative weak image delivered by comments such as "Please! Get away from me!" or "I beg you.... Let me go!"

If you still feel uncomfortable about the idea of speaking so crudely, let me remind you that YOU ARE ATTEMPTING TO PREVENT AN ATTACK ON YOUR LIFE. This is not the time to be prudish or worry about being disrespectful of your religious convictions.

It is not my intention to offend you; I am only trying to help you understand the rules of this deadly game. Please don't take me out of context. I am not endorsing the use of vulgarity in everyday dialogue. I am emphasizing its extreme importance as a **verbal fighting tool.** It has the potential to stop the attack. It is worth a try and will not make your situation any more dangerous.

It is possible your verbal fighting will have no impact on him at all. Maybe he will follow through with the attack as he intended. In this case, although you did not stop the attack, you did allow your adrenaline and anger to be released. This helps build your confidence for the inevitable—physically fighting him. By turning to confront him, you put your body in an excellent fighting position to attack his vital targets (as you will learn in the next chapter).

HE MAY HIDE AND JUMP OUT AT YOU....

This type of attack gives little opportunity for mental preparation. You are going to have to rely on "gut" reaction. The principles for you to remember are:

- **BREATHE!** I guarantee you will be holding your breath!
- **ROAR!** You'll notice I did not say scream. I said ROAR, and there is a difference. When you ROAR, the muscles in your face tighten and you look like an enraged animal. The sound of a roar is atrocious and cannot be misinterpreted to mean anything else but a cry for help! Compare it to the different sounds a dog makes barking at the mailman in the middle of the day and roaring at prowlers in the middle of the night. One is a common sound, generating no reaction at all, and the other signals danger and gets a concerned owner out of bed to investigate the problem.

Before you read on, take time to practice an animal roar so that you can experience just how effective it is:

- Put your hands on your stomach so you can feel your muscles tighten.
- Take a deep breath (inhale).
- Release your breath, bellowing out the most distressed sound you can . . . making sure every muscle in your body is tense (exhale).
- Repeat, making sure you are inhaling and exhaling deeply.

Did you feel the muscles all over your body tighten up? Great! You've got it! Anybody in your house come running to your aid yet? There are five good reasons why you want to roar if attacked:

- **ROARING builds your confidence.** When attacked, the hardest response is often the first response. BREATHE and ROAR! You'll feel confident knowing that you've broken the "freeze" and are reacting to the attack.
- **ROARING affects your attacker's confidence.** The attacker may be startled by your ability to respond so quickly. The anger in your roar and the distressed look on your face will certainly let him know he's in for a fight with an "animal"! It may be more resistance than he cares to gamble with.
- **ROARING helps protect your body.** When you roar, every muscle in your body is tense. These tense muscles create protective "walls" around your vital organs and tighten your stomach cavity. The coupled strength of muscle tenseness and adrenaline pump will allow your body to tolerate more abuse than usual. Tense muscles also help protect you from being "winded" should you be punched, kicked, or slammed to the ground.

  Don't misunderstand my point! AFTER the attack you may feel pain and be badly bruised, maybe even injured; but DURING the attack your endurance level is high, and the pain and injury inflicted upon you won't necessarily stop you from defending yourself.
- **ROARING makes you stronger.** When you tense every muscle in your body while roaring, YOU ARE STRONG! If you strike your attacker with a tense Claw Hand, you can be sure that a tense forearm, shoulder, chest, stomach, and leg is backing up that strike. Don't forget about the additional strength generated by the adrenaline pump in your body.

  Regardless of your size and weight, YOU

ARE AS DANGEROUS AS YOUR MIND WILL ALLOW YOU TO BE, especially when you recognize the devastating strength of your roar and adrenaline!

- **ROARING may alert others that you need help.** Bellowing out a blaring, ear-piercing roar may attract attention. I hope you can generate a loud roar. If you can't, don't be discouraged. I list this as the least important reason for roaring because I recognize that some people are quiet and can't generate volume, especially when they are scared. "Soft roars" are just as valuable as "loud roars." They both increase confidence, strength, and endurance—the volume is just "icing on the cake"!

Remember, if you are ever surprised with an attack, fight back verbally. **Breathe** and **Roar!** Accept the fact that in this type of approach, you will more than likely have to follow up your roar with a physical fight; the attacker is in your **space** and you must fight to escape. The principles of "Fighting Back Physically" are explained in detail in the next chapter.

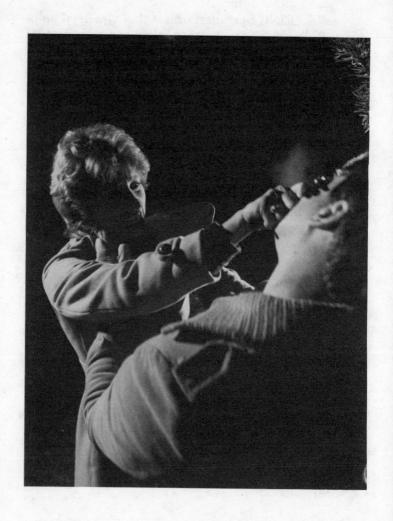

FIGHTING BACK PHYSICALLY

Fighting back physically is not a pleasant thought, but there may come a time when you must face the fact that it is **your only way** to SURVIVE! You tried to outthink him fighting back mentally, and you tried to outtalk him fighting back verbally—but his persistence has pushed the incident to a PHYSICAL CONFRONTATION....IT IS YOU OR HIM!

Here are **six fighting principles** you must always remember:

- **FIGHT PHYSICALLY FOR YOUR LIFE ONLY**— not for property. Your purse or wallet may contain your life's savings but not your life.
- **BREATHE** to control your adrenaline and accept the dangerous situation you are in.
- **ROAR** to increase your confidence, strength, and endurance.
- **HIT FIRST** as he enters your space. It is possible that you may have only one opportunity to strike him. **You must hit him first.** What makes you think you can survive the attack if he hits YOU first? By the way, hitting him first does not turn you into the aggressor in the attack. HE IS STILL THE AGGRESSOR! You are merely defending yourself by protecting your space.

• When you hit, strike with the intention of causing **SERIOUS INJURY,** not just **PAIN.** You must
accept the fact that the person attacking you is
probably "high as a kite" on drugs and/or alcohol.
   These drugs and/or alcohol affect his nervous system, and there is no guarantee that he
feels any pain. When you strike your attacker,
you must hit vital targets with a force that
will cause serious injury and stop his bodily
functions. He will stop his attack not because
he feels pain but because he's lost a vital
function of his body.

• **STRIKE THESE FIVE VITAL TARGETS:**

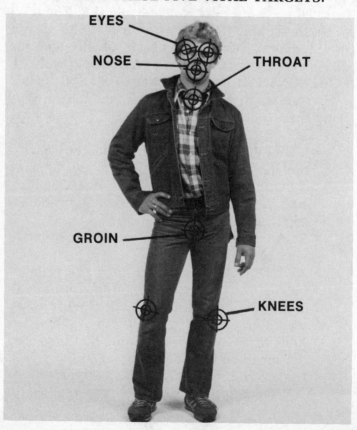

Think of your attacker's head as a "computer," and make your priority targets:

Eyes, Nose, and Throat

Besides causing serious injury, a strike to any of these targets **immediately stops the "computer"** from further calculation against you.

Feel good about your ability to hit at least one of these targets, ANYTIME and ANYWHERE, for these reasons:

- Every human has these targets. Think about it!
- An attacker cannot protect himself by covering them all at one time!

- There are other vital areas of the body, but none is as easily accessible or vulnerable to injury as these.
- No matter what physical condition your attacker is in, these targets are all vulnerable.

These targets are easy to remember. YOU WILL NOT FORGET THEM!

EYES

There is a blinding effect when the eyes are attacked. If he can't see you, he can't hurt you! It only takes a quarter-inch penetration of the eye to cause instantaneous shock.

Does the mere idea of poking eyes make you sick to your stomach? It should! Don't feel bad about it. I don't expect you to like the idea. Poking eyes is a disgusting thought. However, someday if you are desperate, the thought won't even enter your mind.

What if he's wearing glasses? Should you try to reach up under the glasses to attack the eyes? Don't worry about it. Later I describe a Claw Hand attack that harms the eyes and nose simultaneously, thus eliminating the problem.

NOSE

The nose sticks out! Whether your attacker's head is directly in front of you or turned to the side... the nose still sticks out!

The nose is comprised of what I call "little chicken bones" (cartilage) that crush easily. At the very least, an attack to the nose causes temporary blindness. Also, when you crush the nose, those "little chicken bones" puncture blood vessels and cause a tremendous amount of bleeding. Some blood escapes to the outside of the face, but most of the blood falls into the windpipe (trachea), clogging the area and hindering his breathing. If he can't see and he can't breathe, how can he continue attacking you? Remember, he is not going to stop because he feels the injury, he is going to stop because he can't see or breathe!

THROAT

The throat is one of the most vital targets you can hit. Striking the windpipe (trachea) results in internal bleeding and hinders breathing.

Don't think you have to strangle the attacker to cause serious injury. Strike the windpipe forcefully, and you can be sure it will collapse.

The **eyes, nose,** and **throat** are your primary targets. Strikes to these targets **stop** the attacker's "computer" from seeing, breathing, and calculating against you. Striking the next two vital targets is effective in stopping the attacker's bodily functions but may not necessarily stop his "computer" from calculating against you. Think of the next two targets as a means to temporarily disable your attacker until his "computer" is in reach.

GROIN

I'm sure that if you know anything about self-defense, you know to "kick 'em where it hurts." Well, I disagree! Kicking the groin is not as effective as you think. Much emphasis has been placed on the value of this painful strike, but what did I say about pain? He may not feel any pain! An attacker whose body is contaminated with drugs and alcohol will not react to a kick in the groin as would your husband, father, or brother who gets his high from coffee or cola.

Another problem with this strike is that you are assuming that your attacker's groin is easily accessible. It probably is not, unless he walks like he just got off a horse.

So why did I list the groin as one of the five targets to strike? Because a strike to the groin can be effective if you know how to do it properly. In order to guarantee serious injury to the groin, you must drive your knee (or foot) all the way in between his legs and thrust upward. A WEAK STRIKE TO THE GROIN DOES NOT CAUSE SERIOUS INJURY! Injury is caused when your knee crushes the testicles, causing massive hemorrhaging (excessive bleeding). Shock, loss of breath, nausea, vomiting, and unconsciousness may follow. There is a more effective strike to the **groin,** which has fewer limitations: the **Claw Hand** (see page 40). This may sound disgusting, but please keep in mind the seriousness of this topic. In a struggle situation, especially if you are knocked to the ground, there may be ample opportunity for you to reach the attacker's groin with one or both hands. Your intention should be to **grab and pull**...yes, **pull** with all your strength! At that point, you have caused serious injury by crushing and stretching the blood vessels in his groin.

KNEES

The knee is a larger target than you think. A strong kick to the front or either side of the knee will immobilize the joint. The ability to walk or run stops. Keep in mind one problem with this strike. A kick to the knee does not stop the "computer." If you are within arm's reach, he can still continue the attack with his upper body. To be safe, if you kick the knees, kick and run, or kick the knees in conjunction with a Claw Hand strike to his "computer."

Remember, injury to the primary targets (eyes, nose, and throat) **directly** affects the "computer." Injury to the secondary targets (groin and knees) **indirectly** affects the "computer." Strike the groin and knees only when the eyes, nose, and throat are out of reach or as a means to get the attacker to place his "computer" within your reach.

Don't forget: When fighting for your life, you

must **breathe.** Assume you may only get to strike your attacker one time.... You cannot afford for that strike to be ineffective. It's best to **strike the computer** (eyes, nose, and throat). Your intention is to cause him **serious injury** (stop seeing, stop breathing, start bleeding, promote shock), **not just pain!** Don't forget to use your valuable **animal roar**...then **escape** as soon as possible!

WARNING: Do not get caught from behind! Yes, I said "Do not get caught from behind!" I refuse to allow you to think that there are magical A-B-C procedures you can memorize to free yourself if you're caught from behind. I know that there are books available that demonstrate, chapter after chapter, how to escape holds such as bear hugs, headlocks, full nelsons, arm bars, and the like. In my opinion, they are all USELESS...too much to remember too late!

I bet you agree that there are too many holds and too many variable conditions even to attempt to demonstrate all the escape procedures. And even if all the escape procedures could be printed, you'd never remember them all. So what is the answer? Make sure you understand basic fighting principles and apply them to your situation.

(Remember when you were taught the principles of math in the fourth grade? You did not memorize every possible multiplication problem that could ever exist. You merely memorized a formula to use to get the answer such as

$$
\begin{array}{ccc}
4 & 4 & 4 \\
\times 4 & \times 40 & \times 400 \\
\hline
16 & 160 & 1600
\end{array}
$$

These principles have been with you all your life!)

I believe you can retain fighting principles all

your life, too, if you understand why they work. What are the principles that prevent getting caught from behind?

- **PRINCIPLES of FIGHTING BACK MENTALLY**
  Don't be afraid to be afraid! Turn and look at what frightens you!
- **PRINCIPLES of FIGHTING BACK VERBALLY**
  Protect your space! Don't let anyone within your elbow room! ROAR!
- **PRINCIPLES of FIGHTING BACK PHYSICALLY**
  Hit first! Strike the "COMPUTER"! Cause serious injury!

How can you possibly get caught from behind practicing these principles?

In my opinion, understanding *fighting principles* is a much simpler answer to the problem than memorizing volumes of self-defense books and depending on your memory.

Your Personal Weapons

When hitting the five vital targets, use your personal weapons effectively!

HANDS

Your hands are probably your best personal weapons. You are used to using them already. You do not need any fancy training. These weapons are always right at the end of your wrists, available to you all the time.

Your entire hand is a weapon. Spread your fingers out and form a **Claw Hand.**

The **Claw Hand** is used to strike at the attacker's eyes. It is not necessary to strike both eyes—one

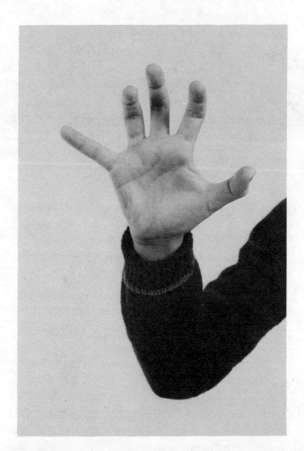

will do. When one is struck, they'll both stop functioning. Thrust out all five fingers toward the eyes. The attacker cannot move his head enough to prevent one of those five fingers from getting at least one eye.

Your **Claw Hand** is also used to strike the nose. The palm of your hand has a large striking surface that can absorb a lot of impact. Thrust your **Claw Hand** into the attacker's nose from any angle. Remember when I said not to worry about glasses? Well, you see that your **Claw Hand** can strike the **nose** and/or the **eyes** simultaneously.

Another use for your **Claw Hand** is grabbing and pulling. Strike the attacker's throat with the **Claw Hand,** grab the windpipe, and squeeze it, attempting to yank it out. That sounds disgusting but not if it saves your life!

Remember what I said about attacking the groin? In order to cause serious injury, you must rupture blood vessels. Your **Claw Hand** can be used to grab the groin, squeeze it, and pull. Then you have caused serious injury, not just pain. I'm sorry to be so blunt. It is not my intention to be crude or disgusting. I just want you to know the truth.

Another hand weapon is to make a **Hammer** with your fists. Never punch your attacker with a boxing-

type punch. (Why do you think boxers wear gloves? Not to protect the other guy's face but their own hands.) Use the bottom side of your **Hammer Fist** to strike the nose. When I say "hammer," I mean like a **Hammer**! You can use your **Hammer Fist** to strike the groin, but remember, to cause injury you'll have to hit...squeeze...and pull.

There are other things you can do with your hand weapons. If you can grab a brick, ashtray, or pop bottle to strike a vital target, do it! Do not restrict yourself when saving your life!

ELBOWS

Elbows are very strong personal weapons. It is extremely difficult for an attacker to grab your elbow or even attempt to block it. The best way to use your elbow is to flex your lower arm as tightly to your upper arm as possible (fist as close to your shoulder as possible).

CORRECT POSITION   **INCORRECT POSITION**

Notice in the first photo that any part of the forearm is also a strong weapon. There is no "give" when it strikes the attacker. You do not have to strike with the elbow bone itself. Elbow refers to the mass area around the elbow point.

Elbows can be used to strike sideward...

upward...and backward.

When striking with your elbows, use your whole body!

KNEES

Knees are similar to elbows. Both are strong, meaty areas of your body that can generate a lot of power. Knee attacks are used to strike **upward,** not **outward.** As with the elbows, flex your lower leg as tightly as you can to your upper leg (your foot as close to your butt as possible). Drive your knee upward with the force of trying to touch your knee to your shoulder. Use your other personal weapons in conjunction with your knee attacks.

FEET

Kicking definitely has its place in self-defense. Not flashy spin or jump kicks, but simple, low, direct kicks. Everybody knows how to kick. You've kicked pop machines when they've stolen your money, right? A basic **Front Kick** is merely a modification of what you already know. When you kick, don't swing your leg up from the floor like a pendulum. That only glances off your target and doesn't have enough force to cause serious injury. In order to cause serious injury, draw your knee up first as if executing a knee attack. From this position, **thrust your foot out** to your attacker's groin or knee with the intention of causing serious injury.

Never kick above your own waist level because you'll lose your balance and strength. Of course, if his "computer" is low, kick it!

The **Back Kick** is exactly what its name implies— kicking straight backward. You know that you should always try to face your attacker, but if you have to fight from a rear angle, this is your strongest kick. Again, **draw your knee up** as if executing a knee attack in the opposite direction. **Thrust your foot straight backward** into your attacker.

Notice that the kicking foot and knee are pointing downward. This affords you the strongest possible kick. While kicking, keep your eyes on the attacker.

The above personal weapons are your primary arsenal (Claw Hand, Hammer Fist, Elbows, Knees, Front Kick, and Back Kick). There are secondary weapons to use should your primary weapons be pinned.

MOUTH

Use your mouth to **roar, bite, and spit.** No matter how distasteful, any blow directed toward his eyes will at least cause a natural reaction of closing or protecting the eyes or moving his head away. This response may be enough for you to strike one of the five vital targets.

HEAD

Use your **Head Butt** to strike the nose.

When using your personal weapons to strike your attacker's vital targets, you must think realistically and accept the possibility of losing your balance and falling or being knocked to the ground by your attacker. If that happens, **do not panic**! You can **SURVIVE** if you know the **principles of falling and groundfighting**.

FALLING

Suppose you lose your balance or you are knocked to the ground by your attacker. Before you can continue to fight back, you must survive the fall by:

- **Protecting your head from smacking the ground.** You cannot fight if you are unconscious from a head injury.
- **Protecting your back.** A back injury might immobilize or even paralyze you.

The principles of falling safely to the ground are:

- **RELAX!** Injuries from falls often occur when people panic and reach for the ground, thereby landing first on bony joints (fingers, wrists, elbows, shoulders, tailbones, and so on). The key to preventing injury is to **relax** and accept the fact that you are going down.

- **TUCK YOUR CHIN** tightly to your chest to prevent a "whiplash" head motion and also to protect your back by rounding your upper spine.
- **DROP YOUR BUTT TO YOUR HEELS.** From whatever position you are in (standing, crouching, squatting), bend your knees, drop your

butt to your heels, and let the fatty tissue of your butt absorb the impact. Dropping your butt as close to your heels as possible protects you from injuring your tailbone.

- **ROLL** to curve and protect your lower spine.

Remember, it is the fear of falling that you need to overcome. No one feels comfortable with the idea of hitting the ground, but sometimes it is inevitable. RELAX, TUCK YOUR CHIN, DROP YOUR BUTT TO YOUR HEELS, and ROLL! Why not stop reading, study the photographs, and try out the principles of falling? You'll see how easy falling safely can be!

A type of fall that does not follow these exact principles is a **Forward Fall.** Should you be tackled from behind (legs pulled out from under you, causing you to fall forward), adjust the principles to fit this type of attack.

- **RELAX!** Don't reach for the ground with your hands—you'll break your wrists. Let your arms bend at the elbow instead, with the back of your hands facing you. Keep your elbows in close to your body, hands level with your face.
- **TURN YOUR HEAD SHARPLY TO EITHER SIDE AND LOCK IT TIGHTLY.** This twist of

your head naturally tightens your neck muscles and prevents whiplash.

• **PROTECT YOUR TORSO.** Fall forward, hitting the ground with your palms and forearms simultaneously. This hand/arm position acts as a "shock absorber" that prevents your torso and knees from hitting the ground first. The fleshy surfaces of your palm and forearm will sting, but your arms will not break.

The thought of falling forward is frightening, but the technique itself isn't that difficult. To help set your mind at ease, start off on your knees instead of

standing straight up. Fall forward, remembering to
RELAX, TURN YOUR HEAD, and PROTECT YOUR
TORSO WITH YOUR "SHOCK ABSORBERS." When
you decide to try it from a standing position, be
sure to protect your knees by locking your legs. If
you let your knees bend, they may be injured when
they hit the ground.

Assuming that you have survived your fall to the
ground, you must begin to fight immediately!

Groundfighting

No one likes the idea of fighting from the ground,
especially if the attacker is still standing. Whether
you've been knocked to the ground or attacked
while sleeping, you can still fight effectively. By no
means should you give up!

- **ROLL UP INTO A BALL** and lie on one side
  or the other, not on your back. Draw your legs
  up tightly into your chest and protect your
  head with your arms.
- **KEEP YOUR FEET BETWEEN YOU AND**

YOUR ATTACKER. As he moves around you, switch from one hip to the other.

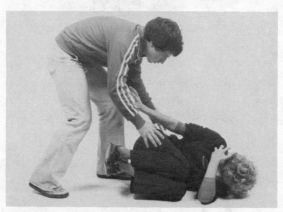

- **THRUST OUT KICKS** to your attacker's knees or groin, one at a time. If he carelessly drops his "computer" down into range, either kick it or strike it with your Claw Hand. Remember to strike hard enough to cause serious injury, not just pain.

Just in case your attacker wasn't disabled or in the case of multiple attackers, you need to get up protected and with good balance.

From your "balled-up" protective position, bend

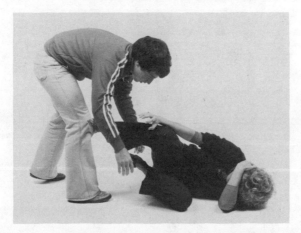

Get up and get away!
But get up right!

the leg that you are lying on and straighten the leg in the air, making a "**4**" position.

Lean toward the bent leg and come up to a half-

standing position. At this point, your balance is good, and your body is protected. Stand and continue fighting until you can escape.

DO NOT use your hands to get up! You need them for protection.

DO NOT get up with your legs crossed Indian style. In that position your balance is poor and you can easily be knocked down again.

Effective **groundfighting** is important for your survival. Have you ever thought how horribly trapped you would be if you didn't resist and allowed the attacker to sit on top of you, pinning your arms, strangling you, or smothering you with a pillow? This desperate situation can be avoided if your groundfighting is effective and you succeed in injuring the attacker before he has the opportunity to trap you.

But just in case you are trapped in this position, here are a few principles to remember:

- **BREATHE** to regain control of your adrenaline!
- **SIMULTANEOUSLY jolt your attacker up and sideways.** Bring in one or both heels as close

to your butt as possible (this gives you leverage), then thrust your hips up off the ground. At the same time, "twist" his balance sideways by thrusting one of your arms toward your head and the other one down toward your hip, turning your body on its side.

This technique works because the simultaneous thrust of your hips and arms causes his balance to be jolted upward and sideways. He cannot regain his body's balance in two directions at one time. In addition, when you are lying on your side, you have more mobility to fight. Bite...pinch...do whatever it takes to break his hold...then strike his vital targets as soon as possible.

If you are attacked while sleeping, an additional principle to remember is to push away the blankets to free your legs. Blankets restrict your movement and can be used to trap you. Pillows can be used to smother you, so knock them aside. Items on your nightstand (lamps, ashtrays, telephone, and so on) can be used in conjunction with your personal weapons to strike your attacker.

Circle Throw

Imagine you are walking down the street and all of a sudden a two-hundred-pound man charges you from around a corner. No matter how effective your strike to his "computer" is, you are going to go down. His forward force will not be stopped by your counterattack. In this case it is likely that you will be injured falling on the ground and having his weight fall on top of you. He is injured by your counterattack, and you are injured by his charging force.

There is a principle to use when confronted with this type of attack. Yield to his charging force by using the **Circle Throw.** (This may appear to be a "flashy" technique. I guarantee it is much simpler than it appears to be. In fact, it can be developed into a natural reaction with very little practice.) When the attacker charges you:

- **ROAR!**
- **GRAB HIS "COMPUTER" to injure and to hold on to him!**
- **AT THE SAME TIME THRUST ONE OF YOUR FEET INTO HIS GROIN to injure and to throw him!**
- **DROP YOUR BUTT STRAIGHT DOWN TO YOUR HEEL and let his force throw himself over you.** You actually have done nothing but attack his vital targets and allow your body to trip him!

He will fall hard on his back **and** be injured from the attack to his "computer" and groin. You will suffer no injury because you fell to the ground on

your own terms—using the safe falling principles you learned earlier. Be sure to get up immediately and escape!

IS IT A THREAT...

...OR A WEAPON?

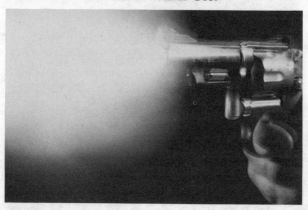

This section is extremely important. Please read it carefully! Then reread it to insure that you fully understand the principles of confronting an armed attacker. By no means is this section intended to provide elaborate instructions, such as what the Secret Service teaches its agents to protect the President. This section is intended to arm *you*, the average citizen, with a couple of sound, working principles that you can recall easily and use effectively when confronted by an armed attacker.

Determine whether the armed attacker is using

that gun or knife as a **THREAT** or as a **WEAPON**! Is there a difference between the two? You bet there is!

When a robber aims a gun at a store clerk and says, "Give me all of your money or I'll shoot you," the gun at that point is being used just as a THREAT. He is using it as an underlying force to get what he wants—money. The robber knows that if he walked up to the counter unarmed, shaking his fist at the clerk and demanding money, the clerk would not take him seriously. Therefore, the robber arms himself with a gun or knife to prove that he is serious and also to frighten the clerk into complying with his demands. In this case, the robber has no intention of using that gun to hurt the clerk; he wants only the money. The gun is being used as a THREAT, not as a WEAPON! The store clerk should not overreact and go after the robber's gun or resist the THREAT in any way. Money is not worth his life!

On the other hand, if an attacker comes into the store, disoriented and wild with rage, walks right past the open cash register and pushes the store clerk into the back room, it is safe to assume that the gun is not being used just as a THREAT—especially when the clerk offers him all the money and possessions in the store and the attacker doesn't appear the least bit interested. The gun in this case is likely to be used as a WEAPON to injure, maim, or kill the clerk. The clerk must react physically to his attacker and the WEAPON. He has no other choice but death. Without a practical defensive plan in mind, you could say the odds of the armed attacker winning in this confrontation are:

Attacker 100–Store Clerk 0

If the store clerk knows just a few fighting principles, he can raise his odds of surviving substantially...but never will he be able to increase the odds to 50/50; that is impossible when one person is armed and the other is not!

I used these examples to emphasize clearly that an armed attacker uses a gun, knife, or the like either as a THREAT or as a WEAPON. If it is being used as a THREAT to get possessions, immediately give up your possessions with absolutely no resistance. If it is being used as a WEAPON, accept that your life is on the line and that you have nothing to lose by using effective principles to survive this armed attack.

Surviving a Knife Attack

(or anything that can cut or stab you, such as ice picks, razors, broken bottles, and so on)

STOP! Put this book down. Go to your kitchen and pick out the sharpest knife you own. NO, I am not kidding! Now, take that knife and lay it across the palm of your hand. Squeeze it tightly and observe: your hand did not fall off! In fact, your hand is not even bleeding. You have just learned a very important principle—knives don't cut just lying across the skin. Knives need a slicing motion to cut. Also, recognize that knives do not cut through bone! It is important that you trust these principles because a successful knife defense depends on your courage to grab the knife! It is not a pretty thought. It boils down to whether you are willing to sacrifice your hand to save your heart or throat. Step by step, let's go through the *fighting principles*.

Assuming you have just been startled by an attacker holding a knife on you:

- **BREATHE DEEPLY to control your adrenaline!**
- **TALK—ask him a direct question. The best is "What do you want from me?"** You have to know immediately if that knife is being used as a THREAT or as a WEAPON. Is it your possessions he wants? If so, GIVE THEM TO HIM! DO NOT RESIST OR ATTEMPT TO OVERPOWER HIM!

Is it your body he wants, as in the case of rape or murder? Make a decision.

Are you willing to give in to rape to save your life?

Do you think pretending to give in to rape will put you in a better fighting position?

Do you think he might kill you anyway, after he rapes you?

Do you think he might kill you first, then rape you?

Do you think he plans to kill you to get rid of a witness to his crime?

These are questions only you can answer. You have to decide whether to give in to rape and take your chances that he'll let you live **OR** decide that you're not willing to give in to rape and choose to fight and take a chance at overpowering an armed attacker when the odds are against you.

Choosing to fight an attacker armed with a

knife means you assume that you'll probably
get cut. You are going to see your own blood.
But you have chosen to have a say-so as to
where the blood is coming from!

Stop and think about how serious this whole
situation is!

- **REACH OUT AND GRAB THE KNIFE BY
  THE BLADE.** Yes, by the blade! You must
  stabilize the knife's movement immediately!
  Squeeze the blade tightly to lessen the knife's
  cutting power. DO NOT ATTEMPT TO WRES-
  TLE THE KNIFE AWAY FROM YOUR AT-
  TACKER. JUST STABILIZE IT AND...

- **STRIKE YOUR ATTACKER'S "COMPUTER"
  WITH YOUR CLAW HAND.**
- **ESCAPE.**

This defense is effective for many reasons:

- Grabbing the knife is totally unexpected.
- Grabbing the knife removes the possibility of
  being stabbed. You may only get cut. This is

very important because a stab will cause your body to go into shock, and the fight will be over. A sliced or stabbed hand will not put your body into shock. A cut hand can be repaired. A stabbed heart cannot!

- Grabbing the knife takes no physical strength. No matter what your size, you can do it.
- Grabbing the knife insures that you are stabilizing its cutting power. It's a more effective defense than grabbing the wrist that holds the knife, as other defense books recommend. When you only grab the wrist, you are not controlling the blade. You can still be stabbed.

Remember, when approached by an attacker armed with a knife, BREATHE, ASK HIM WHAT HE WANTS—IF HE WANTS YOU, STABILIZE THE KNIFE AND ATTACK HIS "COMPUTER," THEN ESCAPE!

These principles apply no matter how the attacker holds the knife on you. The bottom line is that you

accept the fact that you are going to be cut, and you risk your hand to save your life!

Surviving a Gun Attack

Assume that you have already eliminated the possibility of the gun being used as a THREAT to get property. You are now convinced that the gun is going to be used as a WEAPON!

It is important for you to understand that the gun won't kill you (unless you are beaten with it), but the bullet will. Bullets exit from the barrel of the gun; the direction that the barrel is pointing should be your number-one concern. Successful gun defense depends on your ability to grab the barrel and control its direction. Principles of gun defense depend on your being within arm's reach of the barrel. If the attacker is outside of arm's reach, you must close the distance!

The difference between guns and other weapons is that an attacker armed with a gun doesn't have to be close to you to kill you. Attackers are insecure people who use weapons to build their confidence. This means that they are likely to place the weapon against you as a sign of dominance. Little does the attacker know he is doing you a favor...he is putting that barrel within your reach.

The fighting principles of gun defense are:

- **BREATHE DEEPLY** to control your adrenaline and break the "freeze."
- **ASK "WHAT DO YOU WANT FROM ME?"** If you are convinced he is going to shoot you, think...
  How far away is he?
  Is the gun within arm's reach? If it is out of reach, continue talking for the sake of distrac-

tion and shorten the distance by moving carefully toward him. If the gun is held in an awkward position, such as in your back or at your head, deliberately shake your body and pretend to be somewhat hysterical. Acting hysterical for a short period of time allows you to defy his orders ("Don't move....Look straight ahead....") and put your body in a good position to grab the gun.

- **ASSUME THAT AT LEAST ONE SHOT WILL GO OFF!** The critical question is: Where will that shot go? You must protect your "kill zone" by moving it out of the line of fire.
- **REDUCE THE TARGET!** Turn your "kill zone." You may not survive a shot to your head or torso. You can survive a shot to your shoulders,

arms, and legs. By turning, you give the attacker a smaller target.

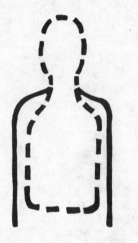

- **REDIRECT THE BARREL.** Yes, **grab it!** Use your hand that is closest to the gun and redirect the barrel. Push the barrel down, up, or to the side, depending on which direction most quickly clears your "kill zone." DO NOT ATTEMPT TO WRESTLE THE GUN AWAY FROM YOUR ATTACKER!
- **STRIKE YOUR ATTACKER'S "COMPUTER" WITH YOUR CLAW HAND!**
- **ESCAPE!**

This entire defense takes tremendous mental courage but is certainly worth the risk if it saves your life. Listed below are the reasons why this defense is so effective:

- Redirecting the gun is totally unexpected.
- Redirecting the gun and turning your "kill zone" greatly enhance your ability to avoid the bullet or survive a shot in a less-vital area.

- Redirecting the gun takes no physical strength. No matter what your size, you can do it!

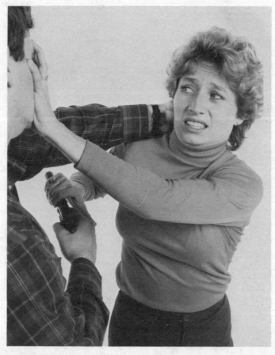

Remember, when approached by an attacker armed with a gun, BREATHE, ASK HIM WHAT HE WANTS —IF HE WANTS YOU, BE SURE THE GUN IS WITHIN REACH. REDIRECT THE BARREL OF THE GUN FROM YOUR "KILL ZONE," ATTACK HIS "COMPUTER" WITH YOUR CLAW HAND, AND ESCAPE!

These principles apply no matter how the attacker holds the gun on you. Assuming that at least one shot will go off, your intention is to increase your odds of surviving. They will never be increased to 50/50. Using these principles to fight, however, your odds will increase to somewhere between 1 and 49, and that is better than 0.

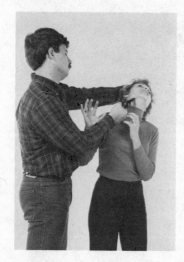 

Here are a few additional principles to consider
when confronted by an armed attacker:

• The best time to go for the weapon is when he
  is distracted. You may think it is hard to

distract the attacker—it is not. Anytime he is talking, he is distracted. Your "action time" (reaching for his weapon) is quicker than his "reaction time" (his response to your defense). When he is talking, his "reaction time" is even slower. The best time for you to **stabilize, redirect,** and **attack with your Claw Hand,** therefore, is when he is talking.

• Do not follow orders given by your attacker once you've established he is going to use that gun or knife as a WEAPON. You must fight immediately. Every order you follow increases his confidence; every order you follow decreases your confidence and can also put you in even more danger.

Example: you are abducted from a shopping center and forced to drive your own car. The armed attacker orders you to drive out of the lot and onto the highway. After driving several miles, he orders you to pull off into a cornfield. Suppose you are able to maneuver an escape. Where are you going to run in a cornfield? Who is going to hear you roar? How much confidence are you going to have left after being dominated by him and his weapon all that time? These conditions all lessen your chance of surviving!

At the initial time of attack, determine exactly what he wants by asking him. Respond accordingly, using the principles you've just learned. In the middle of the shopping-center parking lot, your actions are likely to draw attention, but in the cornfield you'll be all alone! Think about it!

The purpose of an abduction is to take you from a place of activity to a secluded place with absolutely no activity! **DO NOT ALLOW THAT TO HAPPEN!** Your odds of surviving are much better with immediate resistance.

Perhaps you'll feel better dealing with an armed attacker if you understand who uses weapons to commit crimes. With few exceptions, all armed attackers fit one of these four categories.

A "Professional" Robber. This person steals for a living. Unlike you, he does not have a job. When he needs money he'll hold up either a bank, convenience store, gas station, or maybe even YOU! He does not want to hurt you. He just wants your money or other items in your possession. If you resist his demands and struggle with him, he may feel physically threatened, and, in the name of self-defense, he'll use the weapon! All because you wouldn't turn over your possessions. When you ask "What do you want from me?" you can expect this attacker to tell you he wants your possessions. GIVE THEM TO HIM and **end** the attack!

A Desperate, Frustrated Individual. This person has deep emotional problems. He is "at the end of his rope." His frustration and insecurity generally result from a combination of personal misfortunes: unemployment, divorce, separation from children, bankruptcy, and the like. Prior to his personal misfortunes, he may have fit the mold of the average American who worked hard, was devoted to his family, and maybe even went to church on Sunday. Now that his life is in shambles, he has turned to crime because he just doesn't care anymore. This man is not a professional criminal; he is just depressed and feels the need to prove his power and manliness in other ways. He thrives on the idea of controlling others because he's lost the ability to control himself. When he attacks, he uses weapons to demonstrate his power to himself and to his victim. When you ask "What do you want from me?" you can expect this powerless man who is holding a powerful weapon to show signs of nervousness. Maybe he'll stutter when he responds to your question. Maybe his hand holding the weapon will shake. Maybe he can't make up his mind about what he wants. If you recognize these or other signs of insecurity in your attacker, KEEP TALKING TO HIM CALMLY. Play with his conscience carefully. Be sure not to insult him or cause him to go into a rage. Deep down inside he knows right from wrong, and you may be able to say just the right thing to make him stop the attack. Be sure to promise him anything, including your silence about reporting the attack. Then, as soon as you are safe, contact the police immediately!

If talking doesn't stop this attacker's aggression, then you'll be forced to accept your last option: physically defending yourself against the weapon.

A Psychotic, Disoriented Individual. This person "beams" with madness. You'll recognize him immediately. His face is bizarre and twisted; his eyes are wild with rage.

His psychotic condition may be the result of a mental disorder, extreme drunkenness, or excessive drug abuse. His mind is distorted, and his body is out of control. That weapon in his hand is a time bomb waiting to explode!

When you ask him "What do you want from me?" be prepared. He may just stare at you. He may laugh or respond with the filthiest language you've ever heard. DO NOT WASTE YOUR ENERGY TALKING WITH THIS ANIMAL! He is extremely dangerous! Breathe deeply and recognize you have no choice but to defend yourself immediately against the weapon.

An Assassin or Hired "Hit" Man. This person is paid to kill a specific individual, usually a public official or other prominent figure. An assassin calculates and plans every move. He seldom confronts his victim face-to-face. Generally the "kill" is made from a distance with high-powered weaponry or in a terrorist-type ambush.

There is no actual defense against this type of attack. The only encouraging statement I can make about this type of attacker is that his prey is generally not an average person like you or me.

Remember, when confronted by an armed attacker, immediately ask, "What do you want from me?" You need to decide exactly *who* you are dealing with before you can determine *what* your next step must be!

Strangulation

There are two methods an attacker can use to strangle his victim. He can strangle with his hands and arms or use a strangulation device such as an electric cord, rope, coat hanger, or stocking. If he uses his bare hands or arms to strangle you, use your personal weapons to strike his vital targets immediately! (Remember, if you are protecting your space, you are hitting him before he has the chance to grab your throat!) Seconds count when you are being strangled. You will die if you stop to think about anything but striking back immediately!

If the attacker surprises you from behind with a strangulation device around your neck:

- **TURN AROUND AND ATTACK HIM!** Turning is essential. The force of that weapon around the front of your neck is cutting off the air in your windpipe. If you turn around immediately,

that force will be against the back of your neck, and there is nothing back there to strangle! Because you are now facing your attacker, you can strike his vital targets with ease. His hands are "tied up" holding the strangulation device, so he is literally defenseless.

To be quite honest, when an attacker attempts to strangle you, you should assume that he plans to do it with enough force to snap your neck and drag you to the ground. The principle of turning still applies; you can turn while falling, and you can strike his vital targets while falling. The important principle is to protect your windpipe by turning.

NOTE: Your natural reflex before reading this principle probably would have been to reach up and try to pull the strangulation device away from your windpipe. THIS WILL NOT WORK! All you will do is help strangle yourself!

The only logical principle that will save your life when you are strangled is TURN AROUND AND ATTACK!

It would be a good idea for you to stop and practice what you've just read. Ask someone you trust to put a belt (or any other long, wide object) around your neck. Feel how ineffective it is to pull the device away. Then TURN AROUND and feel the release of pressure and also recognize how free your personal weapons are to attack!

Multiple Attackers

Physically fighting multiple attackers should be considered as dangerous as fighting a single armed attacker. No matter what you know or how well you are trained, the odds are not in your favor. Prior to the actual confrontation, be sure you fight mentally with positive body language. If that doesn't deter the attack,

- **BREATHE DEEPLY** to control your adrenaline!
- **IMMEDIATELY FIGHT BACK VERBALLY** by asking "What do you want from me?" If you are lucky, their intention is robbery, and they'll tell you exactly what they want. Do not challenge them! Just give them your possessions and end the attack. If robbery is not their motive, and they want you, accept the extreme danger you are in and rely upon the principles of fighting physically that you read about earlier.
- **POSITION YOUR BODY SO THAT YOUR BACK IS PROTECTED BY A WALL** (or similar cover). Remember, it is difficult to fight off someone who attacks you from behind.

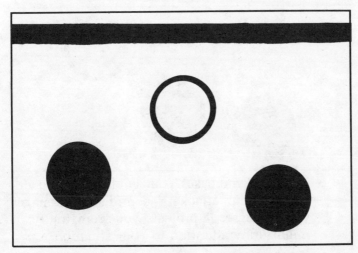

- **FOCUS ATTENTION FIRST ON ANY ONE OF THE ATTACKERS WHO MAY BE ARMED.** He is the most dangerous. Follow through with the weapon-defense principles: stabilize and redirect the weapon; strike the "computer."

- IF NONE OF THE ATTACKERS IS ARMED, the one that is considered the most dangerous is the one closest to you. Before he grabs you, strike him first, making sure you hit a vital target. Turn and strike the next closest attacker, and so on....

- YOU CAN HELP PREVENT THE ATTACKERS FROM GANGING UP ON YOU all at one time by positioning one of them between you and the others.

- If your upper personal weapons (head, hands, elbows) are trapped during the struggle, use your lower personal weapons (knees, feet) and vice versa. **DO NOT LIMIT YOURSELF WHEN FIGHTING: BITE, SPIT, PINCH, PULL HAIR**—do anything it takes to generate the opportunity to hit your attackers' "computers."

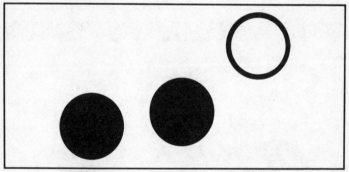

- **ROAR!** It increases your confidence and decreases your attackers' confidence; it makes you stronger; it protects you from injury; it might draw attention to your situation.

Mental determination and solid fighting principles are your only hopes of surviving this type of attack. Unfortunately, there are no other reasonable alternatives.

Weapons You Can Carry

Is there a rash of crime in your neighborhood or town that has you nervous when you are alone? Are you looking for a weapon that you can carry for extra protection? Think rationally about your options.

GUNS OR KNIVES

These weapons are useless unless they are in your hands and you have the courage to use them. They do no good hidden in your car, purse, or coat pocket. Technically you are breaking the law when you carry a concealed weapon, so you must accept the consequences of a police search during a traffic stop or other routine encounter.

When you conceal weapons for your protection, you may be endangering curious people (especially children) who may accidentally discover and experiment with your hidden weapon.

I do not believe that guns and knives are practical defense weapons. I hope you agree.

CHEMICAL MACE

I personally am not convinced that carrying chemical mace (any brand, any size) is valuable in a self-defense situation. The only real credit I can give mace is that it serves as a good awareness tool prior to the attack. Beyond that point, I consider it a "maybe" product:

> Maybe it's held properly when you need it; maybe it's not!

> Maybe it's on; maybe it's off.

Maybe its valve is clogged; maybe it's open.

Maybe it's out of spray because you test it periodically; maybe it's full.

Maybe it will jet-stream 3 feet and hit the attacker's eyes; maybe it will only spray 6 inches and get all over your clothes.

Maybe it gets into his eyes; maybe it just hits his chin.

I think it is unreasonable to risk your life with a product that is so unreliable. When your life is in danger, you may have only one shot at injuring your attacker; don't waste it hurting him with mace. Remember: You must cause serious injury, not just pain, if you expect to survive an attack. Mace, at its best, does not cause injury to the "computer." Striking the "computer" with your personal weapons or other blunt instruments is much more reliable.

NOISE/SHRIEK ALARMS

These items can be put into the same category as mace: "maybe" products. When it comes to noise, depend on your ROAR. It doesn't have to be in your hand, you can't drop it, and it is not limited to batteries or number of squirts to be effective! Whistles fit the same category as noise alarms. A large breath of air is needed to make a substantial noise with a whistle. When you are scared, breathing is going to be your biggest problem. Don't waste your breath blowing a whistle—use it to ROAR! Besides, what reaction will you get from a whistle compared to the sound of your ROAR? Think about it! What do you do when you hear a whistle? I doubt that you would run to investigate a crime, then call the police. You probably would ignore the sound.

KEYS

Keys are part of everyday living. They are needed for just about everything you do. Your keys are probably within reach most of the time. When you are alone, put them to use as a weapon by keeping them in your hand. Putting your keys in between your fingers is one way to use them as a weapon; but a much better use is to put a handle on your keys. There are any number of items that can be used as a handle on your key chain. Just make sure that whatever you choose is long enough to grip comfortably in your hand. Next, make sure that the item itself and the key ring are durable so that your keys don't break off the key ring on impact. The best manufactured handle for your key ring that I know of is a **KUBOTAN**®

KUBOTAN®

Kubotan® was originally invented for police officers as a pain compliance tool useful in controlling suspects. Later a key chain was added to make it more accessible to the officer.

Recently, Kubotan® has been recognized as a valuable self-defense tool for civilians. There are many reasons why I personally value the Kubotan® as an effective self-defense weapon:

- It is easily accessible. Because it is 5½ inches long (6–9 inches with keys attached), it is hard to lose!
- It is durable. The stick is designed to be an impact weapon. It is constructed of solid high-grade plastic that will not bend or break.
- It is highly visible. When you clutch it in your hand, anyone looking can see that you are armed. It definitely improves your body

language. Not only do you look armed, but you also *feel* armed. When you clutch the Kubotan® tightly, there is a sense of security knowing that on the end of your hand you have a weapon that can easily injure an attacker.

• It is an effective weapon. The Kubotan® is actually three weapons in one. Each end is dangerous when thrust at the attacker, and the keys themselves are a perfect flail.

To use the Kubotan® effectively, grasp the handle in the middle.

Swing the keys into your attacker's "computer." Continue jabbing and thrusting the ends of the stick into your attacker's vital targets. Besides the "computer," strikes to the groin are very effective!

Kubotan® is the registered trademark of Takayuki Kubota. For ordering information, write to the Survive Institute, 7265 Kenwood Rd., Cincinnati, OH 45236.

WHO REALLY WINS?

Nothing is more pitiful than consoling the victim of a crime—any crime. Whether it is an elderly victim of a burglary, a middle-aged victim of robbery, a teenage victim of rape, or a juvenile victim of bike theft, each feels disgusted, discouraged, and bitter. The reason? They all know a criminal has scarred their lives, and no matter what they do, they can never realistically make him pay for their damage or scar him back. Victims of crime feel trapped in a "no win" situation.

How about the criminal? How does he feel? Well, if he has been around, he confidently assumes:

"I probably won't get caught."

"If I get caught, I probably won't get charged."

"If I am charged, I probably won't be found guilty."

"If I am found guilty, I probably won't get sent to jail."

"If I do get sent to jail, it probably won't be for very long."

Is crime worth the risk for this man? Of course it is! No matter what he does, the odds are in his favor that he'll escape a lengthy jail term...and he knows it!

Face it—our criminal justice system is a mess! No one has stepped forward with an effective plan to change the system, either. Police officers, defense attorneys, prosecutors, and judges aren't searching for the solutions; they are too busy blaming each other for the problems. The only people who appear to be in control are the criminals!

It is time that you and all good people got angry about this situation and let your opinions be known. Take positive steps to combat crime in your community and let the "ripple effect" lead the way to an improved criminal justice system for all of us. I am urging you to take an active interest in your personal safety and the safety of your community.

- Keep an eye on the judges you elect to work for you. If you are not happy with their conviction rate and sentencing policy, vote them out of office!
- Look at the pay scale of your public employees, especially prosecutors and police officers. If your community pays little, no one will want to protect its citizens. Competent and dedicated prosecutors and police officers don't come cheap. In the midst of a crisis you depend on them to work long hours and produce positive results. Be sure these public servants are being paid fairly so that your community is protected by professionals who know and care about what they are doing.
- Never forget your ability to be as dangerous as your mind will allow you to be. Referring to the previous chapters in this book, depend on the animal in your personality to help you fight effectively to survive an attack.

- Finally, if you ever become the victim of a crime, recognize that an accurate description and the accumulation of physical evidence are the only ways your assailant can be effectively apprehended, prosecuted, and convicted!

A GOOD DESCRIPTION IS ESSENTIAL

When describing your assailant to police, keep in mind that the information they need immediately is a description of his appearance, especially those items that would make him stand out in a crowd. It's going to take your assailant time to get away or change his outward appearance.

When you talk to police, be sure to estimate certain characteristics if you are unsure of an exact description.

Example: If you don't know his exact height, estimate it as "average" or 5′8″–6′1″. This is important because the description you give the police is recorded and becomes evidence in court. If a part of your description turns out to be totally wrong, that small error in your judgment can be used by a fast-talking defense attorney to sway a jury's opinion in favor of his client. "Ladies and gentlemen of the jury, I know there is a tremendous amount of circumstantial evidence against my client, but this police report states that the attacker was five feet eight and my client is six feet one. Now I ask you, how can my client be guilty when he is five inches taller than the described attacker?"

An accurate, incomplete description is more valuable to police than an inaccurate, complete descrip-

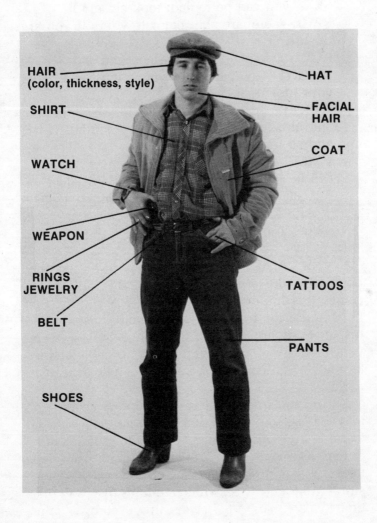

tion. Characteristics you should pay particular attention to are:

SEX—you can be fooled; look closely
RACE—compare skin color to yours if you are unsure
AGE—be vague if you are not sure
HEIGHT—compare it to your own, then make your judgment
WEIGHT—don't give numbers, describe his "build": skinny, medium, stocky, fat, muscular, and so forth
VOICE—was it harsh, loud, soft, deep, or high? Did he have an accent or particular dialect?
PHYSICAL IMPAIRMENT—did he limp or twitch?
SCARS/TATTOOS—give their location, size, shape, and color

If your assailant is not caught within the first hour after the attack, the overall description becomes less important to the police. Assuming that he is out of the immediate area and/or has changed his outward appearance, the police must rely on your memory of such unique unchangeable characteristics as tattoos, scars, speech, or physical mannerisms.

During the investigation of a serious crime, you may be asked to describe your assailant's facial features in depth so that a composite sketch can be drawn. Few police departments actually use artists to draw composite sketches. Most use a device similar to Identi-Kit®, which contains over 350 plastic transparencies of hairstyles, lips, eyebrows, chins, beards, noses, mustaches, glasses, hats, and so on. As you describe specific features in detail (such as rounded chin, bushy eyebrows, wide lips, thin straight medium-length hair parted on the left side, etc.), the investigator chooses transparencies that best match your description; then he overlays them one by one until a complete face is constructed. The accuracy of a composite sketch depends entirely on your determination to study and memorize every feature of your assailant's face.

Identi-Kit® is the registered trademark of Smith & Wesson.

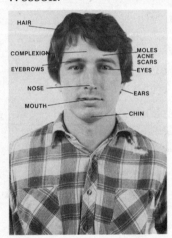

It takes tremendous courage to study the face of someone who intends to hurt you. But you must recognize that an accurate description is essential for police to apprehend and prosecute your assailant. His imprisonment is your retaliation—it is your only guarantee that you personally have prevented him from hurting someone else!

PHYSICAL EVIDENCE IS ESSENTIAL

The lengthy process that starts when the police apprehend your assailant and ends when the judge sentences him to prison is no easy task. You already accept that you are living in a day and age when a criminal's rights are protected while the victim's rights are ignored. In order to counteract this depressing situation, you must build a strong case against your assailant. No one else can do this for you! Make every effort to calculate a deliberate exchange of evidence with him during the attack.

TAKE a part of the criminal and the crime scene with you and LEAVE a part of yourself with the criminal and at the scene of the crime.

TAKE hair from your attacker. Rip it out of his head and hide it in your pocket, up your sleeve, down your pants, in your mouth, ANYWHERE— as long as it is not lost and can be given to police as "his" hair. His hair is evidence!

TAKE skin from his body. Claw and scratch him so that your fingernails are filled with the color pigment and oil content of his skin. His skin is evidence!

TAKE blood from his body. He should be bleeding as a result of your resistance. Smear his blood all over your clothing and other fiber-type surfaces where it can't be wiped away. His blood is evidence!

TAKE personal items off his body. Rip off and hide his loose jewelry, buttons, clothing fiber, and the like. His personal items are evidence!

TAKE pieces of the environment where you've been attacked. Grab and hide any item within reach, such as a dashboard knob, loose seat cover material, carpet fiber, samples of gravel, dirt, grass, leaves, shrubbery, and so forth. Any particle of the environment is evidence!

LEAVE your hair behind. You have plenty of it...pull it out and leave it all over! Place it carefully on your attacker, especially places it is not likely to fall away, like in his pockets. Your hair is evidence!

LEAVE your blood behind. I hope you will be bleeding only from a minor injury. Rub samples of your blood all over the immediate area and also on the attacker's clothing. Your blood is evidence!

LEAVE your jewelry and other personal items behind. Carefully hide a ring down the backseat of his car, leave your watch in the alley, pull buttons off your shirt and leave them in the parking lot. Your personal items are evidence!

LEAVE your fingerprints behind. Deliberately place your finger and palm prints on every smooth surface you can reach. Footprints are valuable, too. Police will use these prints to confirm your presence at the place of your attack. Finger, palm, and footprints are evidence!

LEAVE identifying marks behind. Scratch your initials into surfaces you come in contact with like the seat of car. Claw scar marks into his face. Bite impressions of your teeth into his hand. Identifying marks are evidence!

TAKING and LEAVING physical evidence is critical if you expect to win the war against your attacker. How can he possibly explain the claw marks on his face and the fact that exact samples of his blood, hair, and skin were taken from your body? What excuse can he have for your wedding ring being found in the backseat of his car? How can he explain why the composite sketch you gave the police looks remarkably like him?

With your deliberate accumulation of physical

evidence, you can destroy his assumption about the ineffectiveness of the criminal justice system.

He assumed he wouldn't get caught. He didn't know you had the courage to study his face and make a composite sketch.

He assumed he would never be charged. He didn't know you planted a ring in his backseat for police to locate.

He assumed he would never be found guilty. He didn't know that the prosecutor would present so much physical evidence against him.

He assumed he would never be sent to jail. He didn't know that the jury would be so impressed with the physical evidence that they would not even hesitate to issue a "guilty" verdict.

He assumed he wouldn't be sent to jail for very long. He didn't know he would be sentenced by a newly elected "law and order" judge who gives maximum sentences whenever possible.

Your assailant's apprehension, prosecution, and conviction will depend solely on your courage to *fight back* while accumulating solid evidence and accurate descriptions. **YOU CAN DO IT!** In fact, you owe it to yourself, your family, and your community to *SURVIVE* that attack and go on with your life! See to it that any unfortunate fool who thinks you'll be an easy victim is taught a swift and expensive lesson:

GOOD PEOPLE ARE FIGHTERS, TOO!

When you make sure he **NEVER** desires to commit a crime a second time, then you are the obvious winner. **CONGRATULATIONS!**

Help Yourself with Warner Books

IMPROVE YOUR CAREER
WITH WARNER BOOKS